Paleo Slow Cooker

40 Simple and Delicious Gluten-free Paleo Slow Cooker Recipes for a Healthy Paleo Lifestyle

Sara Elliott Price

Published in The USA by:

Success Life Publishing

125 Thomas Burke Dr.

Hillsborough, NC 27278

Copyright © 2015 by Sara Elliott Price

ISBN-10: 1511850957

Disclaimer

Every effort has been made to accurately represent this book and its potential. Results vary with every individual, and your results may or may not be different from those depicted. No promises, guarantees or warranties, whether stated or implied, have been made that you will produce any specific result from this book. Your efforts are individual and unique, and may vary from those shown. Your success depends on your efforts, background and motivation.

The material in this publication is provided for educational and informational purposes only and is not intended as medical advice. The information contained in this book should not be used to diagnose or treat any illness, metabolic disorder, disease or health problem. Always consult your physician or health care provider before beginning any nutrition or exercise program. Use of the programs, advice, and information contained in this book is at the sole choice and risk of the reader.

Table of Contents

Introduction to The Paleo Diet

This is not a history book, but let me tell you something about the lives of our ancestors in the Paleolithic Era—when there were no malls, no ramen noodles, or canned food. People used stone tools to hunt and capture animals for food. If there was no catch, their families relied on the wild vegetables, tubers, fruit and nuts that were found in season. In other words they ate what humans were meant to eat. They ate food that supports our bodies, and can give us a lifetime of great health.

Many of our ancestors lived long lives and perhaps, died merely because of the dangers of accidents and infections. If you study the primitive cultures that are living today as they have for thousands of years, you find people of robust health with none of the cancer, heart disease or other maladies that affect most of our population today. One of the things that physicians, biochemists, and nutritionists have been studying is the kind of diets that most of us eat today. Grocery stores are lined with packaged junk food, cookies, breads, noodles, sugary drinks—you name it. If you look at this from another perspective, these foods are packed with all sorts of preservative, grains and things that our bodies were never meant to consume. Which is why, the Paleo Diet is quickly becoming the go to lifestyle for not just disease prevention, but overall health. The Paleo diet is our original diet, a diet of whole, unprocessed, and nutrient-rich food.

This kind of diet is not just a fad; it's a lifestyle change, a definite U-Turn. If you want to reduce your risk of all diseases, lose weight and have tons of energy, then this diet is for you. To start living the Paleo lifestyle, first you have to know what foods to eat and what to avoid.

SAY NO TO:

- Grains (Wheat, Barley, Rice, Oats, Corn...)
- Additives
- Starches
- Lentils
- Preservatives
- Refined sugar (such as in sodas or soft drinks, candies, chocolates...)
- Legumes (Soy beans, Peanuts, Chick Peas...)
- Dairy

SAY YES TO:

- Meat (Of grass-fed ruminants)
- Fowl (Chicken, duck, hen, turkey)
- Fish (Wild fish)

- Eggs (The whole egg is a nutritional powerhouse)
- Vegetables
- Oils (Natural oil like coconut, olive, and avocado oil)
- Fruits
- Nuts
- Tubers (Sweet potatoes and yams as alternative to rice and wheat)

The Paleo Diet restricts the use of preservatives, processed food, whole grains, and other toxic food that our modern society consumes in excess. These foods seem to destroy the health of almost everyone who lives in a developed nation.

Grains, preservatives and processed food were not part of our ancestors' diets. Preservatives and processed food contain high amounts of sodium. Sodium works on our kidneys to make our bodies hold on to more water. This extra water stored in our bodies raises our blood pressure and puts strain on our kidneys, arteries, heart and brain.

The Paleo Diet can save you from all the caveats of a modern day lifestyle. The diet of our ancestors can help you build muscle, decrease risks of heart and kidney diseases, boost your immune system, regulate your body clock and sleeping habits, thus, helping you reduce and manage stress. Living a Paleo lifestyle will prime your body to become stronger, healthier, and more resilient in facing bacteria and viruses. If you're new to the Paelo diet just give it a month. You'll notice your clothes may fit better, your skin becomes clearer and you have more energy than you've had in years.

Why We Love Our Slow Cooker

Slow cookers were first introduced by Rival back in 1971. Bean cookers were actually the precursors to the first-ever slow cooker. When people found out the convenience and delicious results of food when cooked slowly, they started modifying models of it. And in 1976, the slow cooker with removable pot inside was invented for easier cleaning and usage.

A slow cooker, also known as a crock-pot, has evolved stylishly in the past few decades, but its functionality remains the same. All you have to do to use it is to place the Ingredients: in the removable pot and set the heat according to the recipe's instructions. Slow cooking usually involves hours of cooking so you may do something else while waiting for your food to cook.

How Slow Is Slow-Cooking?

Dishes that are usually cooked in 15-30 minutes are cooked in 1 to 2 hours on High Temperature or 4 - 6 hours on Low Temperature in slow cooking.

If a dish usually takes 30 to 60 minutes of cooking, it will take to 2-3 hours on high or 5-7 hours on low in a slow cooker.

For dishes that are usually cooked for an hour or two, it would take 3 to 4 hours of slow cooking under high temperature or 6 to 8 hours on low temperature.

SLOW COOKING AND THE PALEO DIET

This way of cooking is very convenient. Since food can be cooked for a couple of hours on low or high heat, you can just leave the food there and the slow cooker will do its job. If you usually go home from work too late and tired to cook for dinner, you can use a slow cooker to prepare your food in the morning so it will be ready to eat in the evening when you arrive home. The convenience aspect is great, but to me I feel the nutritional aspect is even more amazing when you use a slow cooker, especially when it comes to the Paleo Diet. When you slow cook, you can tenderize the Ingredients:—vegetables and meat—without adding any unhealthy additions to the recipe. You do not have to rely on preservatives or seasonings to add flavor to your food. This will generally give you food that is lower in excess fat, sodium, and caloric content.

Since the food in a slow cooker is cooked in one pot without having to remove anything there are very little nutrients lost in the cooking process. Nutrients that would otherwise be lost can even be recaptured, by having the resulting juices or sauces of the recipe included in the meal.

So, you see, there are a number of benefits to slow cooking. In this book you'll find a large assortment of delicious and nutritious Paleo slow cooker recipes. These recipes will leave your taste buds tingling and if you stick with it I think you'll find sticking to the Paleo Diet easier than you ever imagined.

Breakfast Recipes to Start Your Day

Crock Pot Breakfast Casserole

Preparation Time: 20 minutes

Cooking Time: 9 hours

Serving Size: 4-5

Ingredients:

- 1 lb. chorizo sausage
- 1 small onion
- 12 eggs
- 1 cup coconut milk
- 1 small butternut squash
- Ghee/oil for greasing the crockpot

Instructions:

1. Place the chorizo in a skillet, and let it cook.

2. Cut up the onions.

3. Add the onion to the skillet, cooking just until the onion is soft (you don't need to finish cooking the sausage - it will finish in the crockpot).

4. Whip together eggs and coconut milk.

5. Peel, de-seed and dice your squash.

6. Spread ghee/oil on bottom of crockpot to prevent sticking.

7. Add your squash, the sausage/onion mixture and then the egg/milk mixture.

8. Turn crockpot on low for 8-10 hours. Wake up, eat and enjoy!

Maple Blueberry Bacon Breakfast Carnitas

Preparation Time: 30 minutes

Cooking Time: 8 hours

Serving Size: 6-8

Ingredients:

- 1 Tsp. Cinnamon
- 1 Tsp. Dried Parsley
- ½ Tsp. Dried Sage
- ¼ Tsp. Nutmeg
- Salt and Pepper, to taste
- 4 to 5 strips of Bacon
- 2 cups Blueberries
- ¼ cup of Maple Syrup
- Fresh Parsley chopped (to garnish)
- 2 to 3 lb. Pork Shoulder Roast
- ½ cup Apple Juice

Instructions:

1. Set the roast inside the slow cooker and pour the apple juice in, followed by the maple syrup.

2. Sprinkle the nutmeg, salt and pepper, dried sage, cinnamon, and dried parsley on top of the roast. Gently pat with fingers to make sure it stays.

3. Lastly, add a few raspberries to serve as a topping.

4. Cook on low setting for 8 hours.

5. Remove the meat from the cooker and set it aside. Shred the meat.

To help keep the meat moist, add the remaining liquids to the meat.

6. Cook the bacon on the stovetop and place on paper towels to drain excess grease.

7. Once the bacon is cool, crumble it into tiny pieces and add at least half to the shredded pork.

8. Warm your bacon fat pan on medium-high heat and with the help of a large spoon, collect both the bacon and pork. Using your hands press down and form a patty.

9. Press the patty down flat in the skillet and cook each side for about 3 Minutes, until they are nice and crispy. Serve hot.

Paleo Slow Cooker Casserole

Preparation Time: 10 minutes

Cooking Time: 6 hours

Serving Size: 4-6

Ingredients:

- 2 teaspoons of minced garlic
- 1 cup of kale (roughly chopped)
- 2 tablespoons of coconut oil
- 1.5 cups of sliced leeks
- 1.5 cups of shredded sweet potato
- 1.5 cups of beef sausage
- 8 large eggs beaten

Instructions:

1. Melt coconut oil over medium heat in a pan.
2. Add the kale, garlic and leeks and sauté.
3. Add the sweet potato, beef sausage, eggs and sautéed vegetables to your slow cooker, and cook it on low for 6 hours.
4. Let it cool down completely.
5. Divide into equally cut pieces and freeze in freezer bags.
6. To serve, heat in the microwave for about 2 minutes.

Sweet and Savory Sage Stew with Pumpkin and Cherries

Preparation Time: 20 minutes

Cooking Time: 7 to 8 hours

Servings: 4 to 6

Ingredients:

- 2 pounds of grass-fed stew meat, cubed
- 4 cups of butternut squash, cubed
- 1 medium onion, chopped
- 1 cup of dried cherries
- 2 teaspoons of coconut oil
- 1 tablespoon of sage
- 1 tablespoon of thyme
- 1 bay leaf
- 4 cups of beef stock
- 1 teaspoon of allspice
- ½ teaspoon of nutmeg
- 1 cup of pumpkin, pureed
- 1 teaspoon of salt
- 1 teaspoon of ground black pepper

Instructions:

1. In a saucepan, heat the coconut oil and sauté the chopped onions, sage, thyme on medium heat until the onions look translucent.

2. In a high heat skillet, sear the meat until a brown crust forms.

3. Pour the onion mixture and the meat into the crock-pot. Add the beef stock, nutmeg, bay leaf, and allspice. Put this on low heat for 6 hours.

4. After 6 hours, add the cubed butternut squash and dried cherries. Set on low heat for another 1 to 2 hours.

5. Before serving, add pureed pumpkin as desired. Then season with salt and pepper and other spices, if you would like to.

Crockpot Breakfast Pie

Preparation Time: 10 minutes

Cooking Time: 8 hours

Serving Size: 4-6

Ingredients:

- 2 pounds of ground beef
- 8 eggs, whisked
- 2 pieces of sweet potato, shredded
- 1 sweet onion, diced
- 1 tablespoon of garlic powder
- 2 teaspoons dried basil
- 1 teaspoon salt
- 1 teaspoon black pepper
- Any vegetable you want to add (Squash, Chayote, etc.)

Instructions:

1. Add all the Ingredients: (whisked eggs, shredded sweet potato, ground beef, diced sweet onion, garlic powder, dried basil, seasonings, and extra vegetables you might want to include) to your slow cooker and mix well using a ladle.
2. Place on low temperature for 6 to 8 hours.
3. Take it out and let it cool for 5 minutes.
4. Slice it like a pie and voila! It's ready for serving!

Tea Eggs

Preparation Time: 5 minutes

Cooking Time: 4.5 hours

Servings: 5

Ingredients:

- 1 dozen eggs
- 2 to 4 teabags (I enjoy using black tea)
- 6 to 8 cups of water
- 2 tablespoons of cinnamon
- 1 teaspoon of ground black pepper
- 1 teaspoon of salt

Instructions:

1. Place the eggs in a pot filled with water and put on low heat for about 30 minutes or until hard boiled.
2. After the eggs are hard boiled, take them out and place them in a bowl of cold water.
3. Crack the shell of the eggs but do not peel them.
4. Place the cracked eggs in the pot filled with 6 to 8 cups of water. Leave the teabags inside the pot with the strings out and cover the pot with the lid.
5. Let this simmer for about 30 minutes.
6. Remove the teabags and let the eggs simmer for another 3.5 hours with the lid on.

7. Take the eggs from the pot and let them cool. Peel off the shell and place the unshelled eggs in a bowl. Sprinkle salt, black pepper, and cinnamon over them. Serve!

8. You can use a slow cooker for this if desired. Simply leave tea bags with eggs for 2 hours and continue cooking on high heat for 6 more hours. In a slow cooker it will take 8 hours total time.

Slow Cooker Breakfast Meatloaf

Preparation Time: 30 minutes

Cooking Time: 3 hours

Servings: 4 to 6

Ingredients:

- 2 pounds of ground pork
- 1 tablespoon of coconut oil
- 2 cups of sweet onion, diced
- 1 dozen eggs
- 5 tomatoes for slicing
- ½ cup of almond flour
- 2 teaspoons of fennel seeds
- 1 tablespoon of garlic powder
- 2 teaspoons of dried oregano
- 2 teaspoons of red pepper flakes
- 1 teaspoon of ground black pepper
- 1 teaspoon of paprika
- 1 teaspoon of salt

Instructions:

1. Pour 1 tablespoon of coconut oil in a medium sized skillet and place the diced onion over low-medium heat. Cook until onions become translucent. After cooking, set them aside.

2. Combine all the other Ingredients: except the ground pork in a large bowl and mix well by whisking or stirring.

3. Add the softened onions and ground pork to the whisked mixture and use your hands to combine everything well.

4. Gather the mixture in your hands and place in center of your slow cooker. Form the meatloaf, making sure to leave a half-inch of space between the loaf and the walls of the crock-pot.

5. Pat the top of the meat to flatten it and cover the slow cooker with its lid. Slow cook under low heat for about 3 hours. Meatloaf should have an internal temperature of 150 degrees.

6. In a medium-sized skillet, fry the eggs sunny-side up. Once done, place on a plate and set aside.

7. Remove the pot from the slow cooker and let it cool for 15 to 20 minutes.

8. Serve with sliced tomatoes and fried eggs on top.

Lunch Recipes Ready When You Are

Lemongrass Beef Short Ribs

Preparation Time: 15 minutes

Cooking Time: 3 to 4 hours

Serving size: 4

Ingredients:

- 3.5 pounds of beef ribs cut into 5 to 6 pieces
- 5 lemongrass stalks
- 3 - 1 inch pieces of ginger, chopped
- 4 garlic cloves, peeled and smashed
- 1 onion, sliced
- 2 oranges, peeled and juiced
- 1 lime, juiced
- 2 tablespoons of fish sauce
- 1 1/2 cup of water
- Seasonings (Chili flakes, salt, pepper)

Instructions:

1. Place the ribs in the crock-pot and spread out the lemongrass, orange peel, smashed garlic, ginger and onion all around.
2. Pour the orange and lime juice over all the Ingredients: settled on the pot.
3. Pour the fish sauce on top of all ingredients then sprinkle with salt, pepper, and chili for seasoning.

20

4. Pour the 1 and ½ cup of water over all the ingredients in the slow cooker.
5. Cover the slow cooker and set it on low heat for 3 to 4 hours.
6. Serve drizzled with extra lime and orange juice.

Moroccan Chicken

Preparation Time: 20 minutes

Cooking Time: 6 hours

Serving size: 8

Ingredients:
- 3 tomatoes, juiced
- 1 lemon, juiced
- 1 teaspoon of Cumin
- 1 teaspoon of ground Ginger
- 1 teaspoon of Salt
- Half a teaspoon of sweet paprika
- 4 lbs of chicken thighs
- 2 yellow onions, sliced
- 3 garlic cloves, minced
- 3 cinnamon sticks
- 1 to 2 cups of water

Instructions:
1. Mix the juice of the tomato with the lemon juice, cumin, ground ginger, salt, and paprika in a bowl.
2. Preheat a frying pan to a medium high temperature and place the chicken thighs in the pan once heated. Cook the chicken for about 3 to 4 minutes on each side.
3. Once cooked, transfer the chicken into the crock pot.

4. Add the onions, garlic, and ginger to the pan and cook for about 2 minutes. Transfer these to the slow cooker once cooked and the onions are browned.

5. Add all Ingredients: to the slow cooker.

6. Add enough water to cover the chicken.

7. Cover and cook on low for at least 6 – 7 hours.

Slow-Cooker Chicken and Okra

Preparation Time: 45 minutes

Cooking Time: 4 hours

Serving size: 4

Ingredients:
- 4 bone-in chicken legs
- 3 teaspoons organic canola oil
- 4 cloves garlic, chopped
- 2 large onions, sliced
- ½ cup dry red wine
- 3 pieces tomatoes, diced
- 1/3 cup chopped green olives
- 2 bell peppers of any color, cored and sliced
- 3 cups fresh or frozen sliced okra
- ½ cup chopped flat leaf parsley
- 1 teaspoon of salt
- 1 teaspoon of ground black pepper

Instructions:
1. Remove skin of the chicken and season it with salt and pepper.
2. Heat 2 teaspoons of organic canola oil on a large skillet over medium-high heat. Add the chicken and half-cook the legs by turning on each side every 2 minutes. Once done, transfer the half-cooked chicken into the slow cooker.

24

3. Add another teaspoon of organic canola oil to the skillet. Sauté the garlic, onion, salt, and pepper, and cook. Stir often for about 3 minutes until the onions are starting to brown. When finished, transfer this mixture to the slow cooker as well.

4. Pour the wine into the skillet and let it simmer. Stir for about 1 minute.

5. Increase the heat to high temperature and stir in the tomatoes and green olives on the skillet. Allow it to simmer. Pour this mixture over the onions and add peppers to the slow cooker and cover.

6. Turn crock pot on low heat for 8 hours or high heat for 4 hours. Layer the okra on top for the last hour of cooking and remove the lid, as well.

7. Slowly remove chicken and place in individual bowls. Stir the vegetable and sauce mixture together and spread it on and around the meat and top with half a handful of parsley.

Habanero Chili

Preparation Time: 20 minutes

Cooking Time: 4 to 5 hours

Serving size: 5 to 6

Ingredients:

- 1 pound of ground beef
- 1 tablespoon of olive oil
- 1 purple onion, chopped
- 4-5 cloves of garlic, minced
- 1 piece red bell pepper, chopped
- 5 medium carrots, chopped
- 3 stalks of celery, chopped
- 1-2 habaneros, chopped
- 3 tomatoes, diced
- 1 tablespoon of freshly ground black pepper
- 2 teaspoon of oregano
- 1 and a half teaspoon of Cumin
- Salt
- 1 teaspoon of paprika

Instructions:

1. Pour 1 tablespoon of olive oil in a pan or skillet on medium heat. Sauté the onions and garlic.
2. After 2 minutes, add the ground beef and cook until it's browned.

3. Add all the Ingredients:, including the ground beef to a slow cooker and mix them well.
4. Set it on low heat and cook 4 to 5 hours.
5. Serve and garnish with a small amount of celery on top.

Paleo Short Ribs

Preparation Time: 30 minutes

Cooking Time: 8 hours

Serving size: 3 to 4

Ingredients:

- 4pounds of beef, short ribs
- 1 cup of brewed coffee of your choice
- 2 medium sweet onions, sliced
- 4 dried ancho chiles, de-stemmed and de-seeded
- 4 garlic cloves, sliced
- 2 tablespoons of honey
- 2 tablespoons EVOO
- 1 tablespoon lime juice
- Half a cup of water or vegetable broth
- 1 teaspoon of salt
- 1 teaspoon of ground black pepper

Instructions:

1. In a bowl of hot water, set the dried ancho chiles. Leave this for around 20 minutes until they soften.
2. In a food processor, add your garlic, softened ancho chiles, olive oil, brewed coffee, honey, lime and salt and pepper and process.
3. Put the onions in the slow cooker and add your water or vegetable broth.

4. Place the short ribs on top of the onions and pour over the processed mixture of ancho chiles.
5. Season with salt and pepper.
6. Cover with the lid and allow it to cook on low heat for 6 to8 hours. You may also cook it on high heat for 5 to 7 hours.
7. Serve and enjoy!

Enchilada Chicken Stew

Preparation Time: 10 minutes

Cooking Time: 8 hours

Serving size: 4 to 6

Ingredients:

- 2 pounds of chicken breasts
- 1 sweet onion, chopped
- 1 green bell pepper, chopped
- 3 jalapeno, chopped
- 3 chopped green chilies
- 2 tablespoons of coconut oil
- 3 tomatoes, diced
- 3 tomatoes, juiced
- 3 garlic cloves, minced
- 1 tablespoon of cumin
- 1 tablespoon chili powder
- 2 teaspoons dried oregano
- 1 bunch of cilantro
- 1 teaspoon of salt
- 1 teaspoon of ground black pepper

Instructions:

1. Season chicken breasts with salt and pepper and place them in the crock pot.
2. Add all the other Ingredients: on top of the chicken breasts (in any order).

30

3. Set slow cooker on low heat for 8 to 10 hours or high heat for 6 to 8 hours.

4. Use tongs to pick at the chicken and place it on a large plate, allow it to cool for 2 to 3 minutes. Then, shred it in a bowl with all the other Ingredients:.

5. Garnish with cilantro and serve.

Paleo Slow Cooker BBQ Brisket

Preparation Time: 5 minutes

Cooking Time: 10 to 12 hours

Serving size: 6

Ingredients:

- 3 pound of brisket
- 3 tomatoes, diced
- 1 cup of water
- 4 tablespoons of coconut aminos
- 3 tablespoons of raw honey
- 3 tablespoons of apple cider vinegar
- 1 tablespoon of coconut aminos (separately for sauce)
- 1 piece of lime, juiced (separately for sauce)
- Half a tablespoon of cinnamon powder
- Salt

Instructions:

1. Place all the Ingredients:, except the brisket and tomatoes, in a crock pot and mix well.
2. Add the brisket in the crock-pot and cover with the tomatoes.
3. Set the slow cooker on low heat and let it cook for 10 to 12 hours.
4. While slow cooking, prepare the sauce. Mix 1 tablespoon of apple cider vinegar with 1 tablespoon of coconut aminos and lime juice.

5. After cooking the brisket, take out the amount you want to consume. Serve with the sauce.

Paleo Ropa Vieja

Preparation Time: 20 minutes

Cooking Time: 6 hours

Serving size: 6 to 8

Ingredients:

- 3 pounds of flank or side steak
- 2 tablespoons coconut oil
- 1/4 cup of olive oil
- 1 tablespoon of white wine vinegar
- 1/4 cup of basil, chopped
- 1/4 cup of parsley, chopped
- 2 cloves of garlic, crushed
- 5 tomatoes, diced
- 3 red bell peppers, sliced
- 1 tablespoon of onion flakes
- 1 tablespoon of garlic powder
- 1 tablespoon of oregano
- 1 tablespoon of cumin powder
- Salt

Instructions:

1. Slice the steak into two-inch wide strips.
2. Pour 1 tablespoon of coconut oil in a large skillet and pan sear the steak for about 2 to 3 minutes on each side.
3. Place the pan-seared steak in the slow cooker and combine with all the other ingredients. Mix well.

4. Slow cook on low heat for 6 hours.

5. When done cooking, shred the flank steak and mix well.

Ancho Chile Braised Country Style Pork Ribs

Preparation Time: 45 minutes

Cooking Time: 8 to 10 hours

Serving size: 4

Ingredients:

- 5 pounds of country style pork ribs
- 7 tablespoons of ghee
- 4 cups of water
- 6 dried ancho chiles
- 2 dried guajillo chiles
- 6 tomatoes, diced
- 4 tablespoons of apple cider vinegar
- 2 red bell pepper, chopped
- 2 red onion, chopped
- 8 cloves of garlic, sliced thinly
- 2 bay leaves
- Salt
- Pepper
- Cilantro, chopped

Instructions:

1. Cut the ends of the chilies (ancho chiles and guajillo chiles) and remove the seeds. The more seeds there are,

the spicier it will be. So shake off the seeds according to how spicy you want it to be.

2. Toast the chilies in a pan on medium heat and sauté for 2 to 3 minutes. Then let them settle in a bowl.

3. On a separate side, boil your 4 cups of water. After boiling, pour the water over the chilies and let them soak for about 30 minutes.

4. After soaking, pour the soaked chilies and water into a blender and add the pepper, onion, garlic, tomatoes, and apple cider vinegar. Start blending slowly and gradually turn to a higher speed until mixture is completely smooth.

5. Pour half of the chili mixture into a crock-pot and set it on low heat.

6. On a separate skillet, heat the oil over medium high heat and place the ribs in the skillet. Season with salt and pepper. Cook each side for 2 to 3 minutes, allowing them to brown. Place the ribs in the slow cooker.

7. Cover the ribs with the chili mixture and add the bay leaves.

8. Set the crock pot on low heat for 8 to 10 hours.

9. Garnish with cilantro, serve, and enjoy!

Paleo Crock Pot Cashew Chicken

Preparation Time: 20 minutes

Cooking Time: 3 to 4 hours

Serving Size: 4 to 6

Ingredients:

- 2 pounds of chicken breasts, cut into bite-size pieces
- ¼ cup of arrowroot starch
- ½ teaspoon of black pepper
- 1 tablespoon of coconut oil
- 3 tablespoons of coconut aminos
- 2 tablespoons of rice wine vinegar
- 2 tablespoons of organic ketchup
- 1 tablespoon of palm sugar
- 2 garlic cloves, minced
- ½ teaspoon of ginger, chopped
- ¼ cup of pepper flakes
- ½ cup of raw cashews

Instructions:

1. Place the chicken pieces in a bowl and add the starch and black pepper. Mix well and make sure the meat is covered.

2. In a large skillet, heat the coconut oil over medium heat. Place the chicken in the skillet and cook for about 5 minutes. Allow all sides to turn brown by flipping and

turning every once in a while. Once cooked, place the chicken in the crock-pot.

3. In a bowl, combine the coconut aminos with the red pepper flakes. Pour this mixture over the chicken in the crock pot. Set the slow cooker on low heat for 3 to 4 hours.

4. Once done, add cashews on top of the chicken. Then serve.

Chicken Roll-Ups with Prosciutto and Asparagus

Preparation Time: 20 minutes

Cooking Time: 4 hours

Serving Size: 4-6

Ingredients:

- 3 or 4 boneless slices of chicken breasts
- 6 to 8 slices of Prosciutto (Or Spiced Ham of choice)
- 1 bunch of asparagus
- Chopped garlic cloves
- 1 teaspoon of salt
- 1 teaspoon black pepper

Instructions:

1. Slice the chicken breasts into flat and thin slices.
2. Smash your chicken flat with a meat mallet. You can put a piece of plastic on top of the chicken slices while mashing them to lessen the mess and avoid crushing it too much. Smash the chicken on both sides until the chicken is tenderized and ready to roll.
3. Slice your asparagus according to the length of the rolls that you want to make.
4. Lay the asparagus and chopped garlic cloves on top of the smashed chicken breasts and slowly roll it. Make sure that the contents are intact.

5. Roll a piece of Prosciutto or ham around the chicken roll up and use a wooden tooth pick to hold the roll altogether and avoid making a mess.

6. Put the roll ups in the slow cooker and cook on low heat for 4 hours.

7. Take them out of the slow cooker and let them cool. Serve.

Slow Cooker Chicken Breast with Figs & Squash

Preparation Time: 25 minutes

Cooking Time: 6 to 7 hours

Servings: 5 to 6

Ingredients:

- 3 pounds of boneless and skinless chicken breasts
- 15 dried figs, chopped
- 1 cup of butternut squash, chopped
- 1 cup of chicken broth
- 1 cup of vegetable broth
- 1 tablespoon of olive oil
- 1 small red onion, chopped
- 1 small yellow onion, chopped
- 3 garlic cloves, minced
- 1 teaspoon of dried rosemary
- 2 tablespoons of fresh sage, chopped
- 1 teaspoon of salt
- 1 teaspoon of ground black pepper

Instructions:

1. Take a large skillet and pour the olive oil into it. Sauté the onions and garlic over medium heat for 3 to 5 minutes until they are fragrant.

2. Season the chicken breast slices with salt and pepper and place it in the large skillet. Let each side cook for about 5 minutes until they are a little brown.

3. Transfer the chicken and the sautéed garlic and onions to the slow cooker and add the remaining Ingredients: as well.

4. Cook it for 6 to 7 hours on low heat. When done, let it cool for about 5 minutes. And then, serve!

Beef and Mushroom Stew

Preparation Time: 10 minutes

Cooking Time: 6 to 8 hours

Serving Size: 6 to 8

Ingredients:

- 2 pounds of beef stew meat
- Sliced button mushrooms and Portobello mushrooms
- 1 sweet potato, chopped
- 4 garlic cloves, peeled and smashed
- 1 cup of Pearl Onions
- 1 cup chicken or beef broth (Water will also do)
- Half a cup of balsamic vinegar
- 2 tablespoons red wine vinegar
- 1 bay leaf
- 2 tablespoons of onion powder
- 1 tablespoon dried rosemary
- 1 teaspoon dried sage and parsley
- 1 teaspoon of salt
- 1 teaspoon of black pepper

Instructions:

1. Put all the sliced mushrooms, smashed garlic, and pearl onions in the bottom of your slow cooker.
2. Place the meat and sweet potatoes on top.

3. Add the seasonings (salt, pepper, rosemary, sage, parsley, balsamic vinegar, red wine vinegar, and the broth or water).

4. Cook on low heat for 6 to8 hours.

5. Take it out and let it cool for 5 minutes. Serve it up!

Dinner Recipes the Whole Family Will Love

Coconut Curried Chicken Soup

Preparation Time: 30 minutes

Cooking Time: 7 hours

Serving Size: 8-12

Ingredients:

- 4 cups of bone broth
- 2 tablespoons of yellow curry
- 1 knuckle of ginger
- 2 cloves of garlic
- 2 red bell peppers
- 2 carrots
- 2 onions
- 2 tablespoons of coconut oil
- 2 limes
- 8 boneless, skinless chicken breasts
- 4 cups of coconut milk
- 4 tablespoons of almond butter
- ½ cup chopped cilantro

Instructions:

1. Prepare your crock pot and set it on high heat. Drizzle some coconut oil in the bottom of the pot.

2. Grate ginger, mince garlic, dice red bell peppers and onions, and slice carrots. Add these Ingredients: to the crock pot. Mix in the 2 tablespoons of curry. While preparing the other Ingredients:, allow to sauté for 8 minutes.

3. Place the chicken breasts on top of the other Ingredients: in the crock pot. Add in 2 halved limes and the bone broth.

4. Reduce the heat to low and cook for 5-7 hours.

5. After cooking, mix Ingredients: together in a large bowl with the coconut milk and almond butter. Combine them well and add back to the crock pot after mixing. Stir the contents of the crock pot to combine.

6. Remove the chicken breasts from the crock pot and using 2 forks, shred them.

7. After shredding the chicken breasts, return them to the crock pot.

8. Mix the shredded chicken breasts well with the other Ingredients: and taste for desired flavor.

9. Serve your curried chicken soup with lime wedges and enjoy it while it's hot.

Garlic Chicken Wings in Honey

Preparation Time: 15 minutes

Cooking Time: 6 hours if heat is low, 3-4 hours if high

Serving Size: 5-6

Ingredients:

- ½ teaspoon pepper
- ½ teaspoon salt
- 2 tablespoon of garlic
- 2 tablespoon of olive oil
- 1 cup of raw honey
- 3 pounds of chicken wings

Instructions:

1. Mince your garlic and in a small bowl, mix the following Ingredients: well: minced garlic, salt, pepper, honey and olive oil. You can also heat these Ingredients: over the stove in order to soften the honey in case it's very thick.

2. In your crockpot, add the chicken wings. Depending on the size of your crockpot you may not be able to use all 3 pounds of wings.

3. Drizzle your mixed Ingredients: over the chicken wings in the crockpot.

4. Stir Ingredients: together to ensure that the wings are covered in sauce.

5. For 6 hours, cook the wings on low heat. You can also choose to cook them on high heat for 3 to 4 hours.

Paleo Corned Beef and Vegetables

Preparation Time: 25 minutes

Cooking Time: 9 hours

Serving Size: 6-10

Ingredients:

- 2 onions
- 6 carrots
- 1 head of cabbage
- 3 pounds of corned beef brisket with season packet
- 3 cups of water

Instructions:

1. Cut your carrots into chunks. Chop the onions and wedge the cabbage.
2. In a 6-quart crockpot, combine the carrots, cabbage, and onions.
3. Meanwhile, rinse the corned beef brisket under cold running water and pat dry afterwards.
4. Place the corned beef in the crockpot
5. Sprinkle the corned beef with the seasoning mix contents.
6. Pour the three cups of water over the brisket in the crockpot.
7. Cover the crockpot and cook for 9 hours on low heat.

8. Afterwards, remove the corned beef and vegetables from the crockpot.

9. Before serving, cut corned beef into strips and add vegetables to it.

10. Coat the corned beef and vegetables with the juice from the crockpot.

Mushroom Soup

Preparation Time: 10 minutes

Cooking Time: 45 minutes

Serving Size: 4-6

Ingredients:

- Butter
- 2 medium onions
- ½ teaspoon of salt
- 1 pound mushrooms
- Ground black pepper
- 2 teaspoon lemon juice
- ¼ cup chopped parsley
- 1 tablespoon paprika
- 2 cups of chicken broth
- 2 cubed boneless skinless chicken breasts
- 6 cubed boneless skinless chicken thighs

Instructions:

1. Finely dice the onions and slice the fresh mushrooms.
2. Grease a large skillet with the butter and fry the chicken breast and thigh cubes.
3. In a separate stockpot, melt 4 tablespoons of butter. Sauté onions for 5 minutes.
4. Add the sliced mushrooms and sauté for another 5 minutes.

5. Add in the paprika, chicken broth, and cooked chicken cubes into the stock pot and let them simmer for 15 minutes on low heat.
6. Add the black pepper, salt, lemon juice, and parsley to the stock pot and simmer for another 5 minutes.

Shredded Beef

Preparation Time: 10 minutes

Cooking Time: 9 hours

Serving Size: 6

Ingredients:

- 2 pounds of sirloin steak
- ½ cup chicken broth
- 1 large yellow onion
- 1 teaspoon salt
- 1 teaspoon garlic powder
- ½ teaspoon paprika
- ½ teaspoon black pepper
- ½ teaspoon white pepper
- ¼ teaspoon chili powder

Instructions:

1. Slice your yellow onions.
2. Prepare crock pot and set it to low heat.
3. Place the sirloin steak in the pot and add the chicken broth and onions.
4. Add the garlic powder, paprika, salt, black and white pepper, and chili powder.
5. Cover the crock pot and cook for 9 hours.
6. Afterwards, take 2 forks and shred the steak.
7. You can now serve and enjoy your shredded beef.

Coconut Chicken Drumsticks

Preparation Time: 30 minutes

Cooking Time: 5 hours

Serving Size: 4-6

Ingredients:

- Ground black pepper
- 4 cloves of garlic
- 1 ginger
- 1 cup coconut milk
- 2 tablespoon of fish sauce
- 3 tablespoons of coconut aminos
- 1 teaspoon of five spice powder
- 1 large onion
- Salt
- 10 drumsticks

Instructions:

1. Remove the skin of chicken drumsticks.
2. Mince the garlic and thinly slice the onion. Place the drumsticks in a large bowl and season them with salt and pepper.
3. In a separate bowl, combine the garlic, ginger, fish sauce, coconut milk, coconut aminos, and five spice powder. Mix them well until a smooth sauce is formed.

4. Pour the sauce over the chicken drumsticks and mix well.
5. Prepare a crock pot and place the sliced onions into the bottom of the pot.
6. Add the chicken drumsticks into the cooker and marinade it with the sauce you've made.
7. Set the crock pot on low heat and cook for 4-5 hours.
8. When it's done cooking, you can now plate and serve it. Enjoy!

Asian Pepper Steak

Preparation Time: 1 hour

Cooking Time: 7 hours

Serving Size: 6

Ingredients:

- 2 pounds of sirloin steak
- 1 clove of garlic
- ¼ cup coconut aminos
- 2 tablespoons of coconut oil
- 1 large green bell pepper
- 1 small onion
- Salt
- Pepper

Instructions:

1. Mince the clove of garlic and slice the green pepper and onion.
2. On a chopping board, cut the steak into strips of your desired length and thickness.
3. In a large pan, heat the coconut oil. When it's hot, sauté the strips of steak until browned.
4. After sautéing, remove the steak from the pan and drain excess fat.
5. Coat and season the steak with ground pepper.
6. Prepare your crock-pot and set it to low heat.

7. Put the steak in the crock pot and add garlic and tamari. Mix well so that the steak is liberally covered.
8. Cook the meat on low for 6 hours.
9. Afterwards, add the green peppers and onions and turn the heat to high.
10. Cook the steak for one hour on high heat.
11. Serve and devour.

Jambalaya Soup

Preparation Time: 30 minutes

Cooking Time: 6 hours

Serving Size: 3-5

Ingredients:

- 4 red bell peppers
- 1 large onion
- 1 large can of organic diced tomatoes
- 2 cloves of garlic
- 2 bay leaves
- 1 pound large shrimp
- 4 oz. of chicken
- 1 head of cauliflower
- 2 cups of okra
- ¼ cup of hot sauce
- 5 cups of chicken stock

Instructions:

1. Chop the peppers and onion.
2. Dice the garlic cloves and chicken.
3. Drain the juice from the can of tomatoes.
4. De-vein the raw shrimp.
5. Place the chopped peppers and onion, diced garlic and chicken, hot sauce, and bay leaves in the crock pot. Add in the chicken stock.

59

6. Cook the Ingredients: on low heat for 6 hours.

7. About thirty minutes before the Ingredients: in the crock pot are done cooking, make the cauliflower rice by pulsing the raw cauliflower in the food processor until it looks like rice.

8. After making the cauliflower rice, add it and the raw shrimps to the crock-pot.

Apple Pork Tenderloin

Preparation Time: 15 minutes

Cooking Time: 8 hours

Serving Size: 6-8

Ingredients:

- 2 tablespoon of raw honey
- Nutmeg
- 2 pounds of pork tenderloin
- 4 apples

Instructions:

1. Slice the apples and remove cores.
2. Prepare the crockpot and add a layer of apples in the bottom.
3. Sprinkle the apples in the pot with nutmeg.
4. Cut your pork tenderloin in half or whatever size you prefer so it can lay in a single layer in the crockpot.
5. Cut slits in the pork tenderloin.
6. Take one apple slice and place one in each slit in the tenderloin.
7. Place the remaining apple slices on top of the pork tenderloin and sprinkle once again with nutmeg.
8. Set the heat to low and cook for 8 hours.

Crockpot Minestrone Soup

Preparation Time: 15 minutes

Cooking Time: 6 to 8 hours

Servings: 5 to 6

Ingredients:

- 2 tablespoons of EV olive oil
- 2 shallots, diced
- 1 medium sized carrot, diced
- 2 celery stalks, diced
- 1 sweet potato, diced
- 2 zucchini squash, diced
- 2 cloves of garlic, minced
- 2 cups of vegetable broth
- 3 pieces of tomatoes, diced and juiced
- 1 cup of fresh spinach, chopped
- 2 bay leaves
- 1 teaspoon of basil
- 2 teaspoon of dried oregano flakes
- 1 teaspoon of parsley
- 1 teaspoon of ground black pepper
- 1 teaspoon of salt

Instructions:

1. Prepare crockpot and add olive oil.
2. Place together zucchini, sweet potatoes, celery, shallots, carrots, and garlic and the vegetable broth.

3. Add the tomatoes, frozen spinach, oregano, parsley, pepper, salt and basil. Stir.

4. Place the bay leaves on top and cover the pot with its lid. Set it on low heat for 6 to 8 hours.

5. Before serving, don't forget to remove the bay leaf.

Slow Cooker Herb Chicken

Preparation Time: 15 minutes

Cooking Time: 4 hours

Servings: 5 to 6

Ingredients:
- 1 whole chicken (4 pounds)
- 4 medium carrots, chopped
- 1 medium onion, chopped
- ¾ cup of chicken broth (Could be homemade)
- 8 cloves of garlic, divided (2 minced and 6 whole)
- 3 tablespoons of organic olive oil or ghee
- 1 tablespoon of rosemary, diced
- 1 tablespoon of sage, diced
- 1 tablespoon of thyme, diced
- 1 teaspoon of salt
- 1 teaspoon of black ground pepper

Instructions:
1. Place the chopped onion and carrots at the bottom of the slow cooker. Add the garlic and the chicken stock.
2. Place the whole chicken in a large bowl and rub it with oil and season with salt and pepper.
3. Sprinkle the spices and garlic and rub it again to make sure the flavor will seep in.

4. Place the whole chicken in the slow cooker and set it on low heat for 4 to 5 hours. Take the chicken out when cooked and allow it to cool for 5 to 10 minutes. Slice and serve!

Crockpot Cauliflower Bolognese with Zucchini Noodles

Preparation Time: 10 minutes

Cooking Time: 3 ½ hours

Servings: 5 to 6

Ingredients:

For the Bolognese:

- 1 cauliflower head, cut into florets
- 1 piece of red onion, diced
- 2 small garlic cloves, minced
- 2 teaspoon of dried oregano flakes
- 1 teaspoon of dried basil flakes
- 5 pieces of tomatoes, diced and juice (divide)
- ½ cup of vegetable broth
- ¼ teaspoon of red pepper flakes
- 1 teaspoon of salt
- 1 teaspoon of ground black pepper

For the pasta:

- 5 large zucchinis, cut very thinly like noodles (or use a spiralizer)

Instructions:

1. Combine all the Ingredients: for the Bolognese in a crock-pot and set it on high heat for 3.5 hours.

2. After cooking, smash the cauliflower florets with a fork until they break up, creating a "Bolognese" texture.
3. Place the zucchini on a tray and pour over the Bolognese (or you may serve it in a separate bowl).

Slow Cooker Curried Chicken Stew

Preparation Time: 15 minutes

Cooking Time: 4 hours

Servings: 5 to 6

Ingredients:

- 2 pound of boneless chicken thighs
- 4 cloves garlic, smashed
- 1 onion, chopped
- 3 carrots, chopped
- ½ head celery, chopped
- 3 tomatoes, crushed (you may use a blender)
- 1 tablespoon of turmeric
- 1 tablespoon of cumin
- 1 teaspoon of salt

Instructions:

1. Place the chicken thighs at the bottom of the crock-pot.
2. Mound the onion, carrots, celery, and garlic on top of the chicken.
3. Pour the crushed tomatoes over the vegetables and season with salt, cumin, and turmeric.
4. Set the slow cooker on high heat for 4 hours. After cooking, mix well, allow it to cool and serve.

Paleo Dessert Recipes to Satisfy Your Sweet Tooth

Pumpkin Pie Pudding

Preparation Time: 10 minutes

Cooking Time: 6-8 hours

Ingredients:

- 1 teaspoon baking powder
- 3 tablespoon of coconut flour
- 1 ½ tablespoon of vanilla extract
- 2 teaspoon pumpkin pie spice
- ½ cup coconut sugar
- 3 eggs
- 2 cups of coconut milk
- 3 cups pureed pumpkin
- 3 tablespoon of melted coconut oil

Instructions:

1. Grease the inside of the crockpot with a little of the melted coconut oil.
2. Add all the Ingredients: to the crock pot and stir them to combine.
3. Set the crockpot on low heat, cover it, and cook for 6-8 hours or until a crust has formed on top and the edges are browned.

Banana Coconut Foster

Preparation Time: 10 minutes

Cooking Time: 2 hours

Serving Size: 12

Ingredients:

- ½ cup lemon juice
- 4 teaspoons lemon zest
- 1 cup melted coconut oil
- ½ cup honey
- 2 teaspoons of cinnamon
- 2 cups of coconut flakes
- 1 cup chopped walnuts
- 20 bananas
- 2 teaspoons of vanilla extract
- Coconut cream

Instructions:

1. Cut the bananas into quarters.
2. Prepare the crock pot. Place the bananas in the pot and top them with walnuts and coconut flakes.
3. In a bowl, combine together the other Ingredients: except for the coconut cream. Pour the mixed Ingredients: over the bananas in the crock pot.
4. Set the heat to low and cook for 2 hours or until the bananas are tender.

5. Serve on plates. You can pour coconut cream over the bananas and serve.

Apple Butter

Preparation Time: 10 minutes

Cooking Time: 8 hours

Ingredients:

- 2 ½ tablespoons of butter
- ½ teaspoon of nutmeg
- ½ teaspoon of cloves
- 3 tablespoons of cinnamon
- ½ cup pure maple syrup
- 6 apples

Instructions:

1. Dice the apples and prepare the crockpot.
2. Place all the Ingredients: in the pot and mix well.
3. Set the heat to low and cook for 6-8 hours or until the apples are completely mushy.
4. After cooking, remove half of the mixture from the crockpot and put in a blender. Blend until the mixture turns smooth.
5. Afterwards, blend the remaining mixture from the crockpot.
6. When done blending, transfer the mixture to jars using a spoon or a spatula. To preserve, put jars in the freezer.

Slow-Cooked Apple Dessert

Cooking Time: 3 hours

Serving Size: 4 people

Ingredients:

- 4Granny Smith apples, cored
- 2 teaspoons cinnamon
- ¼ cup almond butter
- ½ cup melted coconut butter
- 4 tablespoons unsweetened coconut shreds
- 1 cup water
- ½ cup dried dates
- 1/8 teaspoon salt
- 1/8 teaspoon nutmeg

Instructions:

1. In a bowl, mix almond and coconut butter well.
2. Add salt, cinnamon and nutmeg.
3. In a crockpot, cover bottom with water and put in apples.
4. Fill apples with butter mixture then add dates, a dash of cinnamon and coconut shreds.
5. Cook for 2-3 hours.

Chocolate Drizzled Almonds

Cooking Time: 5 hours

Ingredients:

- 340grams pure dark chocolate, crushed into small pieces
- 1 cup unsalted whole almonds
- 1 cup raw coconut, flaked
- salt

Instructions:

1. Prepare crockpot and line with parchment paper.
2. Arrange almonds evenly in bottom of crockpot.
3. Sprinkle coconut flakes and chocolate over almonds.
4. Cover and cook for 2 hours until chocolate is well melted.
5. Allow to cool uncovered for 3 hours.
6. Place in refrigerator for further cooling and remove from parchment paper to serve.

Buttered Fried Apples with Cinnamon

Cooking Time: 3 hours

Ingredients:

- 8 apples
- 4 tablespoons of butter
- 6 teaspoon of cinnamon

Instructions:

1. Cut the apples into slices, preferably ¼ slices.
2. Place butter in crockpot and let it melt.
3. Once the butter is hot, you can then add the apple slices. Make sure not to overlap.
4. Sprinkle the apple slices with the cinnamon.
5. Cook for 2-3 hours until apples are browned and soft.
6. Serve and devour!

Coconut Apple Crisp

Preparation Time: 3 hours

Cooking Time: 2 hours

Serving Size: 4-6

Ingredients:

- 1 ¼ teaspoons of nutmeg
- 4 ½ teaspoons of cinnamon
- 4 tablespoons of coconut oil
- 4 tablespoons of honey
- 8-10 apples
- ¼ cup butter
- 3 tablespoons of tapioca starch
- 2 tablespoons of coconut flour
- ½ cup of coconut sugar
- 1 cup coconut shreds
- Pinch of salt

Instructions:

1. Prepare crockpot and line with parchment paper.
2. Peel and chop the apples.
3. Prepare a small pan and set it to low heat.
4. In the pan combine the honey, coconut oil, 1 teaspoon of nutmeg, and 4 teaspoons of cinnamon. Melt Ingredients: together.

5. Pour the melted mixture of honey, oil, and spices over the chopped apples and toss to combine.

6. Spread out evenly in bottom of crockpot.

7. In a separate bowl, mix the butter, tapioca starch, coconut flour, sugar, coconut shreds, ½ teaspoon of cinnamon, ¼ teaspoon of nutmeg, and pinch of salt. Combine the Ingredients: until they create a crumbly mixture.

8. Sprinkle the crumbly mixture over the chopped apples.

9. Place the apples in the crockpot for 2 hours or until the topping is browned and crisp.

10. Remove the parchment paper and allow the apple crisp to cool for 15 minutes before serving.

Conclusion

The recipes in this book prove that you don't need to sacrifice taste or time to keep your body fit and healthy. As you can see the delicious Paleo meals you can make with your slow cooker are truly endless.

No longer will you have to rush home to figure out what to cook for dinner. You now have the option of having your meals waiting for you when you're ready to eat. Not to mention how much easier staying on a healthy Paleo diet is when you don't constantly feel stuck in the kitchen.

If you continue to live a Paleo lifestyle you may be amazed at the continued improvements in your health. Your weight will become optimal, your hormone balanced and aches and pains will continue to decrease while living this lifestyle.

In other words you may notice yourself feeling younger as time passes. If you're like me slow cooker meals will be a regular addition to your diet. The amount of time saved creating healthy dishes at home makes it nearly impossible to resist.

Made in the USA
San Bernardino, CA
03 December 2016